How best to teach a beautiful ignorant soul?
Repetition. Repetition. Repetition.
—William Garner

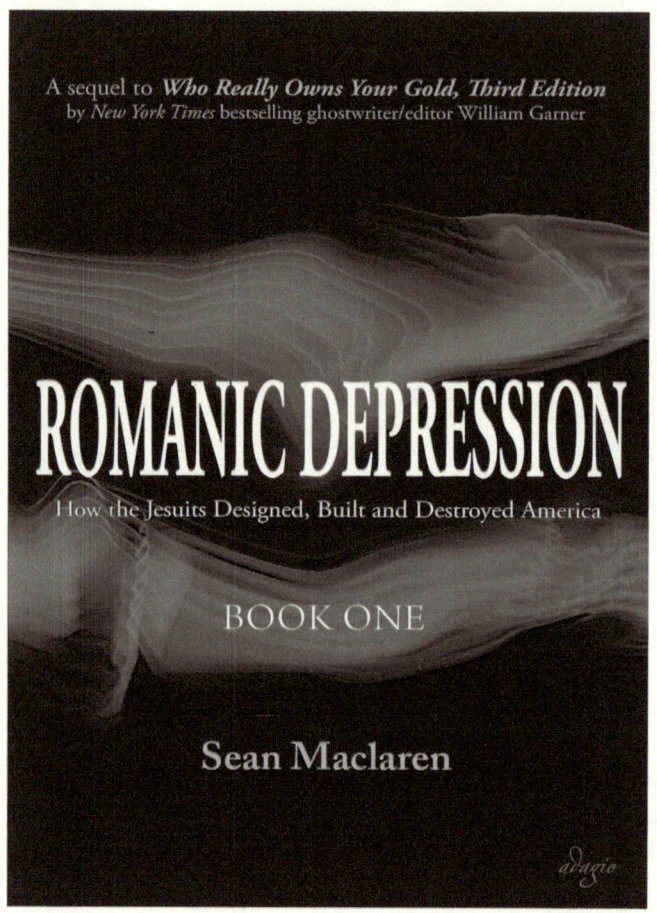

Romanic Depression
Available from Amazon.com and other bookstores

eBook available from Amazon.com, AdagioPress.com and WilliamDeanAGarner.com

The first book in a four-part series that reveals how the Jesuits have designed, built and destroyed every sector of American society, from Law and Government to Politics to Healthcare to Education. Also with more than 200 excellent references.

Edited by William Dean A. Garner
New York Times bestselling ghostwriter/editor

The Suppressed Truth
About the Assassination of Abraham Lincoln
Available from Amazon.com and other bookstores

eBook available from Amazon.com, AdagioPress.com and WilliamDeanAGarner.com

Burke McCarty was a courageous ex-Catholic who conducted diligent research on the details surrounding the murder of President Abraham Lincoln by the Jesuits.

Edited by William Dean A. Garner
New York Times bestselling ghostwriter/editor

Machiavelli's *The Prince*
Available from Amazon.com and other bookstores

eBook available from Amazon.com, AdagioPress.com and
WilliamDeanAGarner.com

The Prince is a raw and bloody field manual for upper- and mid-level managers on predatorial ethics and power: what it is, how to obtain it, and what to do with it once you have found, stumbled across, or been granted it.

Edited by William Dean A. Garner
New York Times bestselling ghostwriter/editor

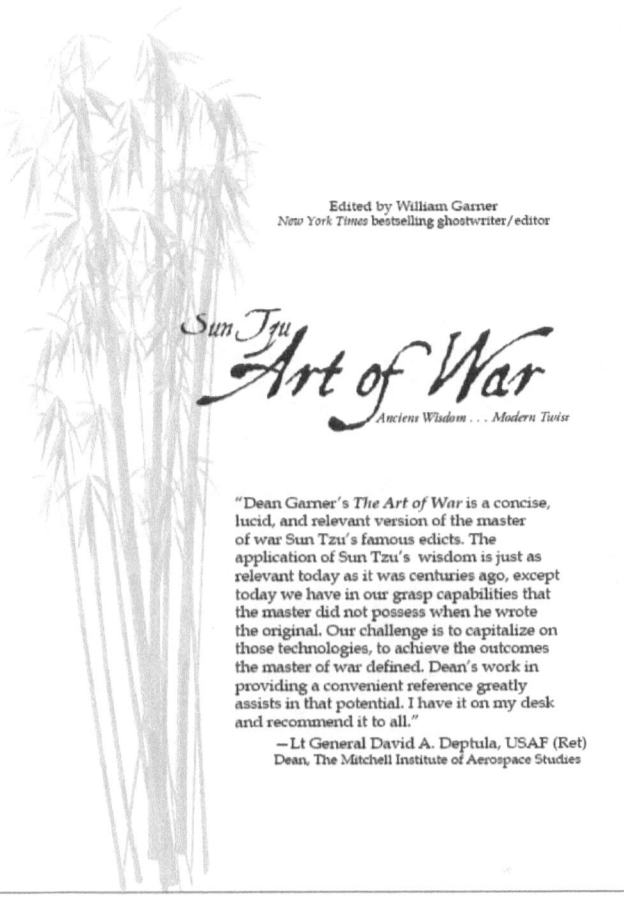

Sun Tzu *The Art of War*
Available from Amazon.com and other bookstores

eBook available from Amazon.com, AdagioPress.com and WilliamDeanAGarner.com

This contemporary edition of Sun Tzu's timeless masterpiece is just as, if not more, relevant today as it was 2,500 years ago, and is wholly effective on the battlefield, and in the boardroom and bedroom. The wisdom of *The Art of War* teaches us that war is unnecessary. Peace is always the goal.

Edited by William Dean A. Garner
New York Times bestselling ghostwriter/editor

The Escape and Suicide of
John Wilkes Booth
The Jesuit Assassin of Abraham Lincoln
Available from Amazon.com and other bookstores

eBook available from Amazon.com, AdagioPress.com and
WilliamDeanAGarner.com

Researcher, author and attorney Finis L. Bates did exhaustive work to uncover the accurate history about Jesuit assassin John Wilkes Booth after he murdered President Abraham Lincoln.

Edited by William Dean A. Garner
New York Times bestselling ghostwriter/editor

Fifty Years in the Church of Rome
Available from Amazon.com and other bookstores

eBook available from Amazon.com, AdagioPress.com and
WilliamDeanAGarner.com

Rev. Charles Chiniquy chronicles his 50 years as a servant of the Church of Rome, while also revealing the evil machinations of the Jesuits and their Roman Catholic minions. He includes information about the assassination of President Abraham Lincoln by the Jesuits, and their controlling the United States and other countries.

Edited by William Dean A. Garner
New York Times bestselling ghostwriter/editor

ARCANUM
A critical analysis of the original 36 sermons of Jmmanuel,
the man known to the world as Jesus Christ
Available from Amazon.com and other bookstores

eBook available from Amazon.com, AdagioPress.com and
WilliamDeanAGarner.com

In Part 1, Maclaren psychoanalyzes Jmmanuel's sermons, which are featured in Part 2. In Part 3, Maclaren reveals The Laws of Creation that Jmmanuel discussed but never actually revealed in depth.

Edited by William Dean A. Garner
New York Times bestselling ghostwriter/editor

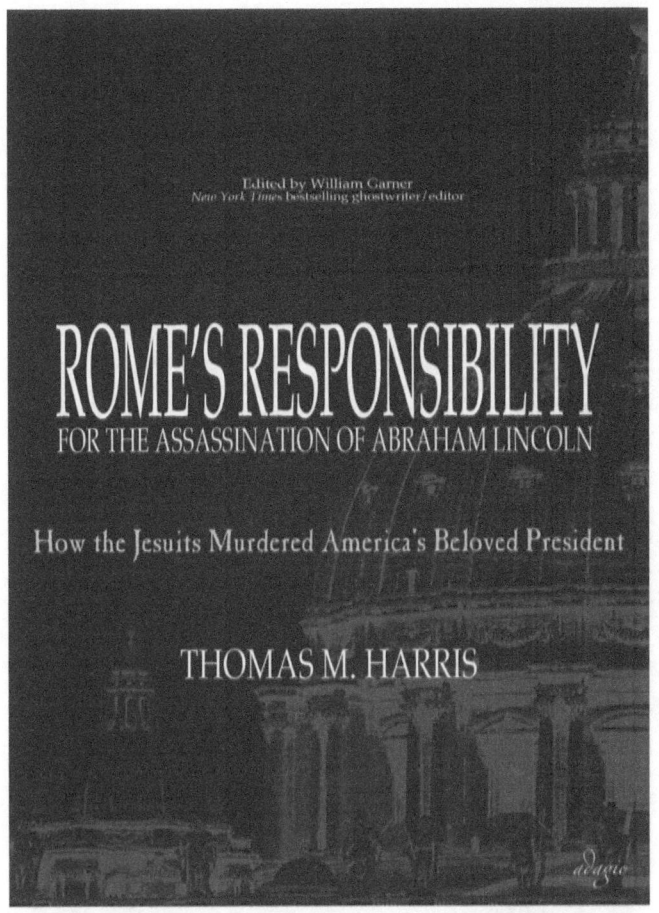

Rome's Responsibility
for the Assassination of Abraham Lincoln
How the Jesuits Murdered America's Beloved President
Available from Amazon.com and other bookstores

eBook available from Amazon.com, AdagioPress.com and
WilliamDeanAGarner.com

General Thomas M. Harris, a member of the Lincoln Assassination Military Commission, details how the Jesuits plotted over many months to murder America's President Abraham Lincoln.

Edited by William Dean A. Garner
New York Times bestselling ghostwriter/editor

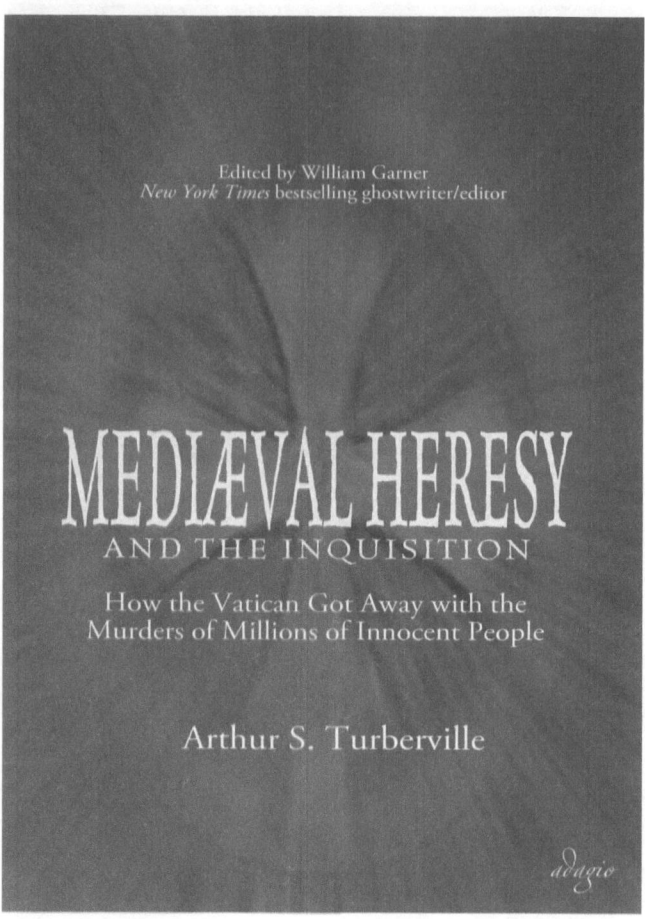

Mediæval Heresy & The Inquisition
How the Vatican Got Away with the Murders of Millions of Innocent People
Available from Amazon.com and other bookstores

eBook available from Amazon.com, AdagioPress.com and
WilliamDeanAGarner.com

Arthur S. Turberville published a fairly detailed account of the infamous Roman Inquisition, a medieval method of torture that was designed to punish and discourage all who opposed the Roman Catholic Church's established dogma.

Edited by William Dean A. Garner
New York Times bestselling ghostwriter/editor

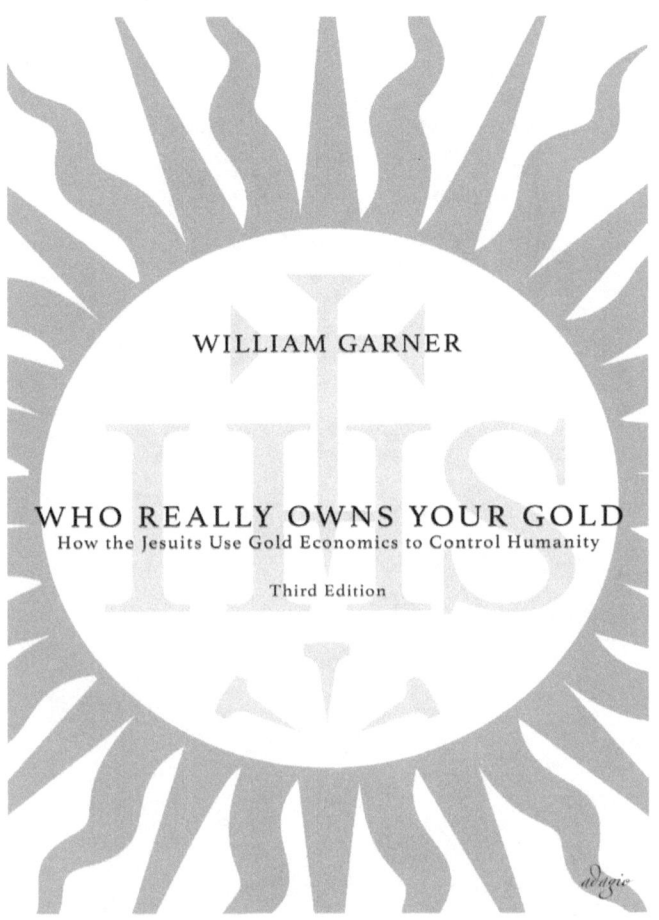

Who Really Owns Your Gold, 3rd Edition
How the Jesuits Use Gold Economics to Control Humanity
Available from Amazon.com and other bookstores

eBook available from Amazon.com, AdagioPress.com and
WilliamDeanAGarner.com

Who Really Owns Your Gold, Third Edition, is about much more than just gold economics. It's about the manipulation of every sector of life across the globe by a dynastic group of men in Rome, the Jesuits, who are successfully building a world that is counter to every good belief we hold dear and true.

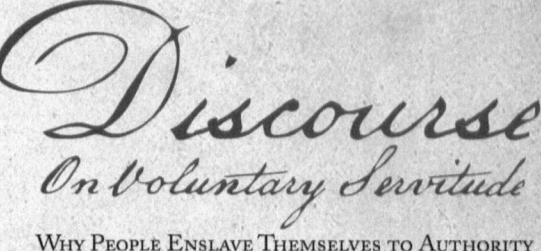

Discourse on Voluntary Servitude
Why People Enslave Themselves to Authority
Available from Amazon.com and other bookstores

eBook available from Amazon.com, AdagioPress.com and WilliamDeanAGarner.com

Étienne de La Boétie's masterpiece is still highly relevant today. While short in words, it speaks volumes to all those who value liberty on all levels, but who are currently trapped in the yoke of oppression by the many tyrants in every government and institution.

Edited by William Dean A. Garner
New York Times bestselling ghostwriter/editor

VA Disability Claim, 3rd Edition
How to Prepare, File and Maintain a VA Disability Claim and Appeal
Available from Amazon.com and other bookstores

eBook available from Amazon.com, AdagioPress.com and VADisabilityClaimBook.com

VA Disability Claim, Third Edition, has been revamped to reflect the hundreds of suggestions from discerning and caring veterans who commented on the first two editions.

Edited by William Dean A. Garner
New York Times bestselling ghostwriter/editor

How To Write Your First Book
A Simple and Practical Method for Anyone Who Can Tell a Story
Available from Amazon.com and other bookstores

eBook available from Amazon.com, AdagioPress.com and WilliamDeanAGarner.com

This gem is much more than just a book about writing. It reveals metaphysically how our subconscious functions during the creative process to produce the finished product, and how we grow spiritually as this process evolves before us to create our first book.

Garner employs a simple, step-by-step method we have used all our lives, and includes easy-to-follow examples and exercises, plus anecdotes from his work as a ghostwriter/editor.

Edited by William Garner
New York Times bestselling Ghostwriter/Editor

The Laws of Creation & The Universe

A Special Gift for Mankind

SEAN MACLAREN

adagio

AN INDEPENDENT PUBLISHING CRUISE
est. January 1, 2001

Katharine L. Petersen
Publisher / Senior Editor

William Dean A. Garner
Editor

Copyright © 2016 Adagio Press
All rights reserved

Published in America by Adagio Press

Adagio and colophon are Trademarks of Adagio Press

Library of Congress Control Number: 2016920953

ISBN: 978-1-944855-08-6

Adagio website: AdagioPress.com

Cover art & design and interior: Dean Garner

B20161225
First Print Edition

for You, dear Reader

Introduction

Welcome to *The Laws of Creation and The Universe*, a brief journey through a complex and difficult yet precious gift from Jmmanuel Sananda, a half-extraterrestrial and half-human being who walked Mother Earth more than 2,000 years ago, presenting sermons and dispensing uncommonly sound wisdom to thousands of disciples and followers.

Much fiction has been written about Jmmanuel, mostly in his more-familiar form as Jesus Christ, including his dying on the cross and being resurrected thereafter.

This book does not seek to correct any of those fictions. There are many excellent books that portray accurately the life of Jmmanuel and his later journeys to the lands of India and Kashmir, where he lived and died well beyond the age of 100 years.

I invite you to explore those books, which are listed in the *References* chapter of this book. There are more than 30 pages of first-rate references for you to discover and research.

All modern religions are based on the sermons of Jmmanuel and *The Laws of Creation and The Universe*.

The various powers and controllers over thousands of years have sought first to control any information about extraterrestrials to Mother Earth and second to suppress any information valuable to humans, especially *The Laws*. Those extraterrestrials who engineered human beings largely have been friendly toward us and have imparted great gifts of wisdom, technology, biology, medicine and philosophy.

Over the years, they have sent us messengers who have given us these gifts in one form or another. In many cases, we humans did not know how to receive these messengers and thus harmed, killed or attempted to control them.

Jmmanuel was the most recent who attempted to impart the wisdom and knowledge of our extraterrestrial engineers. His sojourn on Mother Earth was entirely too short, yet he made every effort to preach the wisdom of his mentors and elders to us in the best way he knew at the time.

Most often, though, Jmmanuel was heavy-handed, arrogant and impatient with us. While he had the extensive knowledge of his mentors and elders, he lacked

Introduction

the ability to share it with human beings in a way they would immediately grasp, understand and use. Seems our extraterrestrial engineers had high expectations of us, and we failed to live up to them.

We are not to blame, though, as we have been programmed over the years to act and conduct our lives in certain ways and according to various powers whose agendas were far different from our own.

In my first book, *Arcanum: A critical analysis of the original 36 sermons of Jmmanuel, the man known to the world as Jesus Christ*, I put Jmmanuel's sermons through a rigorous psychoanalysis, asking hard questions, demanding detailed answers, and, in the end, having to discover many of those answers myself, which is exactly what Jmmanuel had planned all along.

The following is one of the fruits of those labors, the detailed extraction and presentation of *The Laws of Creation and The Universe*, and also the laws and commandments laid down by Jmmanuel and featured on the pages of *Arcanum*.

These *Laws* were loosely preached in sermons by Jmmanuel more during his various sojourns in villages, towns and cities in the Middle East, then later in India and Kashmir, and written and handed down by some of his kin, disciples and scribes.

Curiously, Jmmanuel himself never elaborated on *The Laws of Creation and The Universe*, only tangentially, because he wanted his human followers to extract them from his teachings. In essence, to *earn* them and their precious worth. This was but one of his high expectations of his human followers. Perhaps it has taken this long, more than 2,000 years, to understand, respect and implement his wise words.

Jmmanuel was, to say the least, quite impatient with his human disciples and followers, as they only slowly grasped the meaning behind his words, if they understood them at all. He appeared impatient because he knew his time on Mother Earth was short, and he had only so much of it to impart his wisdom to human disciples and followers.

It also appeared to be his nature, as a half-extraterrestrial being, to expect too much too soon of humans, who clearly were inferior in every way to him and his extraterrestrial family and mentors.

Somehow, though, Jmmanuel knew there existed a handful of special humans, smart and patient thinkers who rose above the average and who would take the time to listen intently to his words and then accurately transcribe them onto scrolls that would survive for thousands of years, only to be discovered only about 50 years ago.

Those who programmed us thousands of years ago ensured we had the necessary tools to survive in harsh climates and endure difficult conditions. They also added special gifts: being *spiritual*. This is not the same as being religious. Having a spirituality is thought to be uniquely human. Perhaps it is.

Being spiritual means reflecting on non-material things greater than we are. This does not entail worshiping any being or object, as with modern religions and their false gods. It means thinking about and meditating on the spirit of The Universe, which fills us all.

That spirit can take many forms. It is up to the individual person, the beholder, to decide what form to think about, talk and share experiences with, pray with, and simply be in the moment with.

I ask that you take quality time to read Jmmanuel's words, absorb their meaning, allow your subconscious to analyze them. In time, they will rise up to the surface of your conscious self and make their presence known. Your subconscious is a most-special gift that serves as the engine for all you do in life. It can be accessed mainly through dreams and dreaming.

During your daily routine, when you read Jmmanuel's words and thoughts, you are actively putting those data into your subconscious, which never rests or sleeps.

When you do sleep, your subconscious is actively considering all the information you sensed and accumulated during the day, distilling it all down to its very essence. The next day or following days, your subconscious then communicates with you via dreams and dreaming to impart what it feels is important to you. You will sense and feel these thoughts through your dreams and daydreams, and begin to act on them.

Further, if you have taken sufficient time to understand them, they will become a part of your very being, allowing you to use them in everyday life without even thinking about them. The process will become so natural that you will find yourself experiencing small (or perhaps large) changes in your own thoughts and behaviors.

These new thoughts will challenge your core beliefs and produce even newer behaviors. After many months of process, you will become a new person, someone you secretly or subconsciously wished to be.

Be patient on your journey. It will take more than mere days, weeks and months to feel some of the changes I described above. The process is slow to start, slower to develop within your subconscious, and even slower to produce concrete results.

You should make a full commitment and see this exciting journey not merely as a set of tools to use in the short run, but as a *lifelong* commitment.

Remember: there is no easy path to *enlightenment*, a full understanding of who you are as a person and human being, what life is about in all aspects, and how the world and all in it function harmoniously to create a small part of The Universe.

I wish you well on this magnificent journey, with the hope you will share it with those you love and care about and with your friends and neighbors, colleagues and acquaintances, and strangers and casuals. . . .

The Laws of Creation & The Universe

- *The Laws of Creation and The Universe* shall forever be observed, as they represent true physical and spiritual events that provide an accurate system of rules governing all forms of matter and energy
- Everything is connected to everything else in The Universe
- There is never one without the other, even good and evil
- The two parts of the spirit are wisdom and power. A person cannot have a healthy spirit without both entities, so one must continually strive to study and understand oneself as best as humanly possible through experiential experience and learning from one's mistakes, thus gaining wisdom over

time. Power comes with exercising wisdom correctly so a person attains further wisdom and power
- Without wisdom of the spirit, its power cannot be utilized, nor can any wisdom emerge without spiritual power
- Greatness, excellence and beauty rule harmoniously where nature is left to itself
- The human spirit is immortalized through rebirth or reincarnation, where the active spirit is passed on to the next living body, entity, or form of matter or energy to further its experiences and knowledge
- You must live your life to the fullest, to the very end of your days
- Blessed are those who are rich in spirit and recognize the truth, for life is theirs
- Blessed are those who endure hardship, for they shall thus recognize truth and be comforted
- Blessed are the spiritually balanced, for they shall possess knowledge. For humans, being spiritual does not mean worshiping a religious entity. It is about studying what comprises the spirit, building on that knowledge, practicing how to improve and grow it, and sharing it with all in life
- Blessed are those who hunger and thirst

for truth and knowledge, for they shall be satisfied. Actively seeking answers to all the questions we have inside us is key to becoming knowledgeable and wise
- Blessed are those who live according to the laws of nature, for they live according to the plan of Creation. We have inside the blueprint for living, and sometimes it is called "common sense." We must live our lives according to what feels natural deep inside us
- Blessed are those who have a clear conscience, for they need not fear
- Blessed are those who know about Creation, for they are not enslaved by false teachings. Simply ignoring the false religions of the world is the first step toward enlightenment
- Blessed are the righteous, for nature is subject to them
- Blessed are you if, on Jmmanuel Sananda's account and because of his teachings, people revile and persecute you and speak all manner of evil against you. Thus they lie about the teachings
- Be of good cheer and take comfort that this life and the next life will reward you
- Smile, laugh, be positive in all interactions, for they are contagious and will spread far

- You are the salt of the Earth, and if the salt loses its flavor with what would one salt? It is useless henceforth, except it be thrown out and stepped on by the people
- You are the light of the world, and consider: the city that lies on top of a mountain cannot be hidden. People are greatly attracted to those who are "lights" and who possess the strength of character to smile, laugh, be positive through the most difficult times. They serve as a beacon of hope for others and an example of how to live a full life
- One does not light a candle and place it under a bushel, but on a candlestick. Thus it shines for all those who are in the house
- Likewise your light shall shine before the people, so they see your good deeds and recognize the truth of your knowledge
- Exercise justice according to *The Laws of Creation and The Universe*, so that you find the judgment in logic. This entails being fair and just with all others, treating people and animals with respect
- Guilty are all those who kill when not acting in self-defense or according to legal verdict based on self-defense. Likewise, guilty are all those who engage in evil speech and action
- Only justice according to *The Laws of*

Creation and The Universe produces a logical judgment
- Do not accommodate your adversaries if you are in the right
- You will attain justice only when you find it yourself and can make your fellow humans understand it
- Give to them who ask of you, if they make their requests in honesty, and turn away from those who want to borrow from you in a dishonest way
- Practice love and understanding according to *The Laws of Creation and The Universe*, so that through logic you find the right action and perception
- Over the course of incarnations, you shall train your spirit and your consciousness and allow them to develop to perfection, so that you become one with Creation
- Choose your words using natural logic, and draw upon the knowledge and behavior of nature
- When you give alms, you shall not proclaim it, as do the hypocrites in the synagogues, churches and on the streets, so they may be praised by the people. Their alms serve only their selfishness
- When you pray, you shall not be like the

hypocrites, who enjoy standing and praying in the synagogues, churches and on the corners of the streets, because they pray only for the sake of their selfishness and the impression they have upon the people
- When you pray, you shall call upon the omnipotence of the spirit and not babble misleading nonsense like the idol-worshipers, the ignorant and the selfish, because they think they are heard when they use many words
- When you pray to your spirit, it will give you what you request. Have trust in this knowledge and you will receive
- Do not amass great treasures on Mother Earth, where moths and rust consume them and thieves break in and steal them, but collect treasures in the spirit and in consciousness, where neither moths nor rust consumes them and where thieves neither break in nor steal
- Collect treasures in the spirit and in consciousness. Where your treasure is, there your heart is also, and the true treasure is wisdom and knowledge
- No one can serve two masters. Either he will hate the one and love the other, or he will adhere to the one and despise the other

- You cannot serve your good spirit and the devil of covetousness. Concern yourself about the knowledge of your spirit and what you will eat and drink, and be concerned about your body and how you will clothe it. The birds in the sky do not sow, they do not reap, they do not store their food in barns, and yet Creation feeds them
- If you suffer from hunger, thirst and nakedness, then wisdom and knowledge will be crowded out by worry. First seek the realm of your spirit and its knowledge, and then seek to comfort your body with food, drink and clothing
- Judge not falsely, lest you be falsely judged. For with whatever judgment you judge, you will be judged, and with whatever measure you measure, you will be measured. Judge according to the logic of the laws of nature, which are from Creation, because only they possess its truth and correctness
- Through *The Laws of Creation and The Universe*, learn first how to recognize your own faults, so that you can then correct the faults of your neighbors
- Do not throw your spiritual treasure into the dirt and do not waste it on the unworthy, because they will not thank you and will

tear you apart, for their understanding is small and their spirit is weak
- Ask, and it will be given to you
- Seek and you will find
- Knock, and it will be opened to you
- Everything that you wish people would do to you, do likewise to them
- The path to damnation is broad, but the path to life and knowledge is narrow, and there are only few who find it
- Beware of false prophets and scribes who come to you in sheep's clothing, but inwardly are like ravenous wolves, preaching to you about submissiveness before shrines, false deities and gods, and preaching submissiveness to idols and false teachings
- Beware of those who forbid you access to wisdom and knowledge, for they speak to you only to attain power over you and to seize your goods and belongings
- Turn away from the false teachings of the Israelite, Roman Catholic, and Muslim authorities, and all their principals, disciples and scribes, because they will bring destruction to successive generations. The Israelites believe themselves the chosen people. By no means is this the case, because they are more disloyal and unknowing than

the ignorant who lack the secret of *The Laws of Creation and The Universe*
- The unrighteous and the ignorant, including the scribes, priests and the authorities, will hate those who have the knowledge and, therefore, will persecute them and sow enmity
- The path of truth is long and the wisdom of knowledge will only penetrate slowly
- This Earth can nourish and support five hundred million people of all human populations. But if these laws are not followed, in two times a thousand years there will exist ten times five hundred million people, and the Earth will no longer be able to support them. Famines, catastrophes, worldwide wars and epidemics will rule the Earth. Earth humans will kill each other, and only a few will survive
- Do away with enforcing the old law that subjects woman to man, since she is a person like the man, with equal rights, responsibilities and obligations
- Take on the burden of having to learn the new teachings of *The Laws of Creation and The Universe*, for they offer enlightenment. Within them you will find peace for your life, because the yoke of spiritual development is

gentle, and its burden is light
- Humans must first experience much guilt and error before they learn to accumulate knowledge and wisdom, so as to recognize the truth
- *The Laws of Creation and The Universe* have been valid for yesterday and today, and therefore for tomorrow, the day after tomorrow, and for all time. Thus *The Laws* are also a determination and hence a predetermination for things of the future that must happen
- Nowhere is a prophet valued less than in his own country and in his own house
- Never doubt the power of your spirit and never doubt your knowledge and ability when logic proves to you *The Laws of Creation and The Universe* in truth and correctness
- The human spirit is ignorant until it has gained knowledge through thinking, inquiry, experience, and implementing those lessons learned
- The spirit of a person is not a human product but is a part of Creation given to humans. It must be made knowledgeable and perfected, so that it proceeds to become one with Creation, since Creation, too, lives

in constant growth
- Those who search, seek and gather insights and thirst for knowledge like a child will be great in spirit. Those who search, seek and find like such a child will always reach their fullest potential within themselves
- There is no sense in life and no fulfillment of its meaning without searching, seeking and finding
- Creation is timeless, and so is the human spirit
- Even when humans burden themselves with mistakes, they act according to *The Laws of Creation and The Universe*, because they learn from them and gather insight and knowledge, whereby they develop their spirits, and through their spirits' strength they are able to act
- Without making mistakes, it is impossible to gather the logic, insight, knowledge, love and wisdom necessary to develop the spirit
- When one makes a mistake that serves the insight, knowledge, and progress of the spirit, there is no punishment, neither in this life nor in any subsequent life. Humans live with the mission of perfecting their spirits and obtaining insight and knowledge through mistakes, so that they

may lead the lives according to their destiny
- Because humans at this time are beginning to think and perceive, they are in need of the teachings. Thus the prophets have been sent by the celestial sons to teach humankind about *The Laws of Creation and The Universe*, and the knowledge regarding life
- Humans are still ignorant and addicted to the false laws of the chief priests and distorters of the scriptures. They do not recognize the new teachings as truth. Lacking understanding, the people curse the truth which yet must come, and they curse, stone, kill and crucify the prophets. But since the teachings of the truth must be brought to the people, the prophets have to bear great burdens and suffering under the curse of the people
- It is better to let an unreasonable person walk on the path of misery than to bring confusion to one's own consciousness
- The heavens will collapse before an unreasonable person can be taught reason
- Whatever a person may wish to accomplish, they must always first create the will to do so, because this is the law of nature
- A person determines the course of their life, known as fate, but they are also bound by

universal laws that govern destiny
- The highest directive in *The Laws of Creation and The Universe*: Achieve the wisdom of knowledge, so that you may wisely follow *The Laws*
- The spirit of each person is created specifically for the task of perfecting itself and gaining wisdom, and sharing this wisdom collectively
- Whatever a person may wish to accomplish, they must always first create the will to do so, because this is the law of nature. Thus a person determines the course of their life, known as fate. Destiny also serves as an active guide to those who obey its laws. One must acquire knowledge and learn the truth to engender a will that is imbued with *The Laws*
- It is easier to bear an adversity with one or two others at one's side than by oneself
- Be awake and great in spirit and in consciousness so you will not fall prey to temptation. The spirit is willing but the flesh is weak
- It is also customary among humans that the most righteous person does not find justice, because it doesn't matter whether many or few testify against him, as long as they are

highly regarded
- A human being shall never attempt to force the truth onto another, because then it would only be worth half its value
- First, humans shall tend to their own progress in consciousness and spirit, so as to produce Creational harmony within themselves
- No greater darkness rules within humans than ignorance and lack of wisdom
- Greatness of personal victory requires uprooting and destroying all influences that oppose the Creational force, so that which is Creational may prevail
- Humans should develop within themselves the power to judge over good and evil and to correctly perceive all things, so that they may be wise and fair and follow the Laws
- It is necessary to be cognizant of what is real and what is unreal, what is valuable and what is worthless, and what is of Creation and what is not
- Humans gain experience in the use of their powers and capabilities only by trying daily to unlock and use them
- There may be no limits to love, peace and joy, because the present state must always be exceeded

The Laws

- Truly, I say to you, a love that is unlimited, constant and unfailing is unconditional and is a pure love, in whose fire all that is impure and evil will burn
- *The Laws of Creation and The Universe* are not hidden from the wise man, hence he can recognize and follow them
- The wise understand that the secret of Primeval-Creation lies in the number seven and in computations based thereon. Thus they will gather and retain the knowledge that Creation has a time for work or rest that is also based upon the number seven
- All things in The Universe are bound together by the number nine and its multiples, whose secrets have yet to be revealed to humans on Mother Earth
- When a blind man leads another blind man, both will fall into the pit
- *The Laws of Creation and The Universe* are also a determination and hence a predetermination for things of the future that must happen
- Although humans have free will to exercise authority over themselves, they do not have the right to decide over life or death
- Every guilt and every mistake is a pathway to understanding by which the consciousness

and the spirit are perfected
- Just as *The Laws* and directives of Creation are the Laws and directives for the spirit and for life, so the laws and commandments of god are the laws and commandments for material life and human regulations
- The extraterrestrial god issued *The Laws* and commandments to serve as material life and human regulations for that which is right, and also as a guideline for life and living
- *The Laws of Creation and The Universe* are to be obeyed, humans must not bring forth any other laws and commandments
- When humans deviate from these laws and directives, however, they bring forth illogical and inadequate human laws and commandments that are based on false logic and, thus, are faulty
- Humans must disregard false teachings and not arrogantly pursue greed for power and fortune
- Man-made laws and commandments produce murder and all manner of evil and, as evil spreads and gains the upper hand, humans no longer have control over it
- Commandments and laws are valuable only when they are derived from wisdom, and hence are logical, but logic requires wisdom

and understanding
- Human laws and human commandments are powerless, unless they are founded upon *The Laws of Creation and The Universe*, just as god's laws and commandments are founded upon them, as he issued them in his wisdom. When humans are presumptuous and disregard *The Laws of Creation and The Universe* and those of god, they are forced to bring forth their own laws that are flawed and lead everyone astray
- Wisdom must be learned from *The Laws of Creation and The Universe*, which humans may recognize in nature. Therefore, seek the comforts of nature and her gifts
- If humans do not think and seek, they will not be able to attain wisdom and will remain fools
- The wise do not moan about lost things, about the dead and about events of the past
- Fools, however, cry over things that are not worth crying over, and thereby they increase their grief, privation and misery
- Those who have acquired sufficient wisdom and live according to *The Laws*, permit not even the slightest harming of creatures, when they are without fault
- Half-wits and fools who are not masters

over their senses mistake harm for benefit, benefit for harm, and great sorrow for joy
- Because people are not dedicated to wisdom and do not seek knowledge or recognize *The Laws*, they harbor foolishness and vice
- The dishonest, the stupid, grumpy, greedy, unscrupulous, uncouth and the angry will suffer harm for being poor in consciousness
- When people duly receive daily just a little wisdom in their consciousness, they will grow like the waxing moon during the first half of the lunar month
- Wisdom is the greatest asset of humanity and so is the created will, which is lord over love and happiness. But all of this is meaningless without the power of the spirit
- A fool who idly rests and waits for fate or destiny without actively participating in life goes to ruin like an unfired pot in water
- Those who take care of a cow always receive milk. Likewise, those who nurture wisdom and apply it through the power of the spirit bring forth rich fruit
- Recognize each *Law of Creation and The Universe* and, once you have recognized it, adhere to it and live accordingly, because *The Laws* are the greatest wisdom
- There is no eye equal to wisdom, no darkness

equal to ignorance, no power equal to the power of the spirit, and no terror equal to the poverty of consciousness
- There is no higher happiness than wisdom, no better friend than knowledge, and no other savior than the power of the spirit
- Those who have intelligence may grasp my speech so they will be wise and knowing
- *The Laws of Creation and The Universe* state: Only that which is timeless and everlasting is of permanence, of truth and of wisdom

Afterword

When you read and absorb Jmmanuel's words, and also the thoughts and interpretations of his work in my book *Arcanum*, hopefully, you will come away with a new understanding of the simple rules of life:

    Be kind and gentle to yourself.

    Live a good, clean life.

    Learn all you can about yourself and all that life has to offer.

    Treat others and animals and all life with respect and dignity.

    Continue to learn and make mistakes, and pass on your lessons learned to others. There is much power when common interests are shared among parents and children, brothers and sisters, and fellow friends and colleagues.

Nothing in these basic rules calls for worshiping any

false God, idol or monument, as specified by current false religions and cults, although the majority of humans on this planet do just this.

The human spirit is easily led down the easy path of darkness. It takes a strong and courageous person to walk the much narrower path of righteousness.

The Laws of Creation and The Universe do tell us all to respect everything in life. There is a world of difference between worship, which is a false order proclaimed by false religious leaders and their followers, and that espoused by *The Laws*: *respect*.

Above all else, *respect yourself and others*.

Whatever happens in your life thereafter follows naturally if you adhere to this simple rule, and also understand and respect the absolute fact that everything on Mother Earth and in The Universe are connected by the smallest unit of matter, the quantoretto, which forms a seamless liquid, or sliq, that binds us all as one.

Everything is intimately connected. . . .

"If we encounter a man of rare intellect, we should ask him what books he reads."
—Ralph Waldo Emerson

References

Books about Jmmanuel Sananda traveling to and living in Kashmir and India, and various accounts of his death and resurrection.

Abbot, S (1917). *The Fourfold Gospels*. Cambridge University Press, Cambridge.

Abdul Qadir bin Qazi-ul Qazzat Wasil Ali Khan (n.d.). *Hashmat-i-Kashmir*, MS. Number 42, Asiatic Society of Bengal, Calcutta.

Abhedananda, S (1987). *Journey into Kashmir and Tibet*. Ramakrishna Vedanta Math, Calcutta.

Abu Jaffar Muhammad bin Jarir at-Tabri (1880). *Tafsir Ibn-i-Jarir at-Tabri (Jami al Bayan fi Tafsir-ul-Qur'an)*, Volume 3. Kubr-ul-Mar'a Press, Cairo.

Abu Muhammad Haji Mohyud-Din (1903). *Tarikh-i-Kabir-i-Kashmir*. Suraj Parkash Press, Amritsar.

Agha Mustafai (1868). *Ahwali Ahalian-i-Paras*. Tehran.

AI-Haj Mumtaz Ahmad Faruqui (1973). *The Crumbling of the Cross*. Ahmadiyya Anjuman Isha'at-i-Islam, Lahore.

Allcroft AH (1917). *The Circle and the Cross*. Macmillan, London.

Allen BM (1919). *The Story Behind the Gospels*. Methuen, London.

Andrews A (1906). *Apochryphal Books of the Old and New Testaments*. Theological Translation Library, London.

Ansault A (1894). *La Croix avant Jésus-Christ*. Paris.

Arbuthnot J (1900). *A Trip to Kashmir*. Calcutta.

Augstein R (1972). *Jesus, Menschensohn*. Gütersloh, Munich; Bertelsmann, Vienna.

Avicenna (n.d.). *Canon of Avicenna*. Newal Kishore Press, Lucknow.

Bacon BW (1918). *The Four Gospels in Research and Debate*. New Haven, Conn.

Baigent M, Leigh R, and Lincoln H (1983). *Holy Blood, Holy Grail*. Harper and Row, New York.

Balfour E (1885). *The Cyclopedia of India and of Eastern and Southern Asia, Vol. 1, 3rd Edition*. Bernard Quaritch, London.

Ball JA (1973). The Zoo Hypothesis. *Icarus*, 46, 347-349.

Barber P (1953). *A Doctor at Calvary*. New York.

References

Bardtke H (1952). *Die Handschriftenfunde am Toten Meer.* Berlin.

Bardtke H (1958). *Die Handschriftenfunde am Toten Meer: Die Sekte von Qumran.* Berlin.

Bardtke H (1962). *Die Handschriftenfunde in der Wüste Juda.* Berlin.

Barth, K (1982). *The Theology of Schleiermacher* (Ritschl D, Editor; Bromiley G, Translator.) Eerdmans, Grand Rapids, MI.

Basharat A (1929). *Birth of Jesus.* Dar-ul-Kutab-i-lslamia, Lahore.

Bauer, B (1850-1). *Kritik der Evangelien,* Volumes I and II. Berlin.

Bauer W (1971). *Orthodoxy and Heresy in Earliest Christianity.* Fortress Press, Philadelphia.

Baur FC (1847). *Kritische Untersuchungen über die Kanonischen Evangelien.* Tübingen.

Beare FW (1981). *The Gospel According to Matthew.* Harper & Row, San Francisco.

Bell AW (1897). *Tribes of Afghanistan.* Bell, London.

Bellew HW (1880a). *The New Afghan Question, or Are the Afghans Israelites?* Croddock, Simla.

Bellew HW (1880b). *The Races of Afghanistan, Being a Brief Account of the Principal Nations Inhabiting That Country.* Thacker, Spink & Co., Calcutta.

Bellinzoni AJ (1992). The Gospel of Matthew in the Second Century. *The Second Century* 9, 235-256.

Bengalee SMR (1946). *The Tomb of Jesus*. Muslim Sunrise Press, Chicago.

Berna K (1957). *Jesus nicht am Kreuz gestorben*. Verlag Hans Naber, Stuttgart.

Bernier F (1891). *Travels in the Moghul Empire* (A. Constable, translator). London.

Bernier F (1916). *Travels in the Mogul Empire (AD 1656-1668)*, 2nd Edition (Constable A, Translator; Smith VA, Editor). Oxford University Press, Oxford.

Beruni-Al (1888). *Indian Travels*, Volumes I and II (Sachan E, Translator). Trubner, London.

Beskow P (1985). *Strange Tales about Jesus: A survey of Unfamiliar Gospels*. Fortress Press, Philadelphia.

Betz O (1960). *Offenbarung und Schriftforschung der Qumrantexte*. Mohr, Tübingen.

Biblioteca Christiana Ante-Nicena, 25 Volumes (1869). Clark, Edinburgh.

Biscoe CE (1922). *Kashmir in Sunlight and Shade*. London.

Blinzler J (1959). *El proceso de Jesús*. Editorial Litúrgica Española, Barcelona.

Blofield J (1977). *Compassion Yoga*. George Allen & Unwin, London.

Blomberg CL (1997). *Jesus and the Gospels*. Broadman & Holman, Nashville, TN.

References

Blomberg CL (2001). The Synoptic Problem: Where we stand at the start of a new century. *Rethinking the Synoptic Problem* (Black DA and Beck DR, Editors). Baker Academic Grand Rapids, MI.

Borg MJ (1993). Me & Jesus: The Journey Home. *The Fourth R*, 6-4 (Jul/Aug), 3-9.

Borg MJ (1990). The Jesus Seminar: Voting Records. *Forum* 6(Mar. 1990) 3-55.

Bornkamm C (1968). *Jesus von Nazareth*. Stuttgart.

Bowersock GW (Ed.) (1970). *Philostratus, Life of Apollonius* (Jones CP, Translator). Penguin Books, Baltimore.

Boys HS (1886). *Seven Hundred Miles in Kashmir*. Church Mission Congregation Press, Calcutta.

Braun H (1957). *Spätjüdisch-häretischer und frühchristlicher Radikalismus: Jesus von Nazareth und die essenische Qumrânsekte*. Tübingen.

Braun H (1962). *Gesammelte Studien zum Neuen Testament und seiner Umwelt*. Tübingen.

Braun H (1966). *Qumran und das Neue Testament*. Tübingen.

Brioton E (1958). *Las Religiones del Antiguo Oriente*. Andorra.

Brown RE and Meier JP (1983). *Antioch & Rome*. Paulist Press, New York.

Bruce CG (1911). *Kashmir. Peeps at Many Lands series*. Black, London.

Bruhl JH (1893). *The Lost Ten Tribes, Where are They?* Operative Jewish Converts Institution Press, London.

Bryce J (1856). *A Cyclopaedia of Geography Descriptive and Physical, forming a New General Gazetteer of the World and Dictionary of Pronunciation.* Richard Griffin and Co., London.

Buchanan C (1912). *Christian Researches of Asia.* Ogle, Edinburgh.

Buhl F (1908). *Canon and Text of the New Testament* (Macpherson WJM, Translator). Clark, Edinburgh.

Bultmann R (1921). *Die Geschichte der synoptischen Tradition.* Gottingen.

Bultmann R (1926). *Jesus.* Tübingen.

Bultmann R (1957). *Das Verhältnis der unchristlichen Christus Botschaft zum historischen Jesus.* Exegetica. Tübingen.

Burke OM (1976). *Among the Dervishes.* Octagon Press, London.

Burkett D (2004). *Rethinking the Gospel Sources.* T & T Clark International, London.

Burkitt FC (1906). *The Gospel History and its Transmission.* Clark, Edinburgh.

Burkitt FC (1910). *The Earliest Sources for the Life of Jesus.* Constable, London.

Burkitt FC (1924). *The Four Gospels, A Study of Origins.* Macmillan, London.

References

Butler BC (1951). *The Originality of St. Matthew.* The University Press, Cambridge.

Butler BC (1969). *The Synoptic Problem. A New Catholic Commentary on Holy Scripture* (Fuller RC et al., Editors). Nelson, Nashville, TN.

Cadoux CJ (1948). *The Life of Christ.* Pelican, London.

Chadurah KHM (n.d.). *Waqiat-i- Kashmir or Tarikh-i-Kashmir.* Muhammadi Press, Lahore.

Chatterjee JC (1911). *Kashmir Saivism.* Srinagar.

Chwolson D (1910). *Über die Frage, ob Jesus gelebt hat.* Leipsiz.

Clark J (1998). *The UFO Book: Encyclopedia of the Extraterrestrial.* Visible Ink Press, Detroit, MI.

Clemen C (1911). *Der geschichtliche Jesus.* Giessen.

Cole HH (1869). *Illustrations of Ancient Buildings in Kashmir.* W.H. Allen, London.

Conselmann H (1968). *Grundriss der Theologie des Neuen Testaments.* Munich.

Conybeare FC, Editor (1912). *Eusebius, Against Apollonius of Tyana by Philostratus. The Life of Apollonius of Tyana, the Epistles of Apollonius and the Treatise of Eusebius*, Volume II. Harvard University Press, Cambridge.

Cook E (1899). *The Holy Bible with Commentary.* John Murray, London.

Cools PJ (ed.) (1965). *Geschichte und Religion des Alten Testaments.* Olten.

Cope L (1976). *Matthew: A Scribe Trained for the Kingdom of Heaven..* Catholic Biblical Association of America, Washington, D.C.

Craig WL (1985). *The Historical Argument for the Resurrection of Jesus during the Deist Controversy.* Edwin Mellen Press, Lewiston, NY.

Danielov J (1959). *Qumran und der Ursprung des Christentums.* Mainz.

Dautzenberg G (1970). *Der Jesus-Report und die neutestamentliche Forschung.* Müller, Wurzburg.

de Quincey D (1903). *The Apocryphal and Legendary Life of Christ.* Nathan, New York.

Deardorff JW (1986). Possible extraterrestrial strategy for Earth. *Quarterly Journal of the Royal Astronomical Society* 27, 94-101.

Deardorff JW (1987a). Examination of the embargo hypothesis as an explanation for the Great Silence. *Journal of the British Interplanetary Society* 40, 373-379.

Deardorff JW (1987b). Extraterrestrial communications. *Journal of Communication*, 37, 181-184.

Deardorff JW (1989). Pleiades pendulum (Letter). *International UFO Reporter* 14 (5, Sept/Oct), 21.

Deardorff JW (1992). *The Problems of New Testament Gospel Origins.* Mellen Research University Press, New York.

References

Deardorff JW (1994). *Jesus in India.* International Scholars Publications (University Press of America), Bethesda, MD.

Deardorff JW, Haisch B, Maccabee B, and Puthoff HE (2005). Inflation-theory implications for extraterrestrial visitation. *Journal of the British Interplanetary Society* 58, 43-50.

Denys FW (1915). *One Summer in the Vale of Kashmir.* James William Bryan Press, Washington, DC.

Derrett JDM (1982). *The Anastasis: The Resurrection of Jesus as an Historical Event.* P. Drinkwater, Shipston-on-Stour, England.

Desjardins M (1991). Bauer and beyond: On recent scholarly discussions of Airesis in the early Christian era. *The Second Century* 8, 65-68.

Dibelius M (1919). *Die Formgeschichte des Evangeliums.* Tübingen.

Docker EB (1920). *If Jesus Did Not Die on the Cross: A Study of the Evidence.* Robert Scott, London.

Dodd CH (1963). *Historical Tradition in the Fourth Gospel.* Cambridge.

Dorn B (1829). *History of the Afghans: Part 1 & 2* (Translated from the Persian of Neamet Ullah). J. Murray, London.

Doughty M (1902). *Through the Kashmir Valley.* Sands, London.

Douglass E (2001). Why doesn't the US government tell the truth about UFOs? *MUFON UFO Journal* 393(Feb), 6-7.

Drew A (1926). *Le Mythus du Christ.* Paris.

Drew F (1875). *The Jammoo and Kashmir Territories*. Edward Stanford, London.

Dummelow JR (1917). *Commentary on the Holy Bible*. Macmillan, London.

Dungan DL (1999). *A History of the Synoptic Problem*. Doubleday, New York.

Dupont A (1959). *Les Éceits esseniens découverts près de la Mer Morte*. Payot, Paris.

Dutt JC (1879). *The King of Kashmir*. Bose, Calcutta.

Edersheim A (1906). *The Life and Times of Jesus*. London.

Edkins J (1890). *Chinese Buddhism*. Kegan Paul, French and Trubner, London.

Edmunds AJ (1900-1). *Gospel Parallels from Pali Texts*. Open Court Publishing, Chicago.

Edmunds AJ (1908-9). *Buddhist and Christian Gospels*. Innes, Philadelphia.

Edwards WD, Gabel WJ, and Hosmer FE (1986). On the physical death of Jesus Christ. *Journal of the American Medical Association* 255(11), 1455-1463.

Ehrman BD (1997). *The New Testament: A Historical Introduction to the Early Christian Writings*. Oxford University Press, New York.

Ehrman BD (2004). *A Brief Introduction to the New Testament*. Oxford University Press, New York.

References

Eifel EJ (1873). *Three Lectures on Buddhism*. Trubner, London.

Eissfeldt O (1964). *Einleitung in das Alte Testament*. Tübingen.

Eliot HN (1849). *History of India as Told by its Own Historians*, 8 volumes. Thacker, Spink and Co., Calcutta.

Emerson ER (1885). *Indian Myth*. Trubner, London.

Esler PF (2005). *Rome in Apocalyptic and Rabbinic Literature. The Gospel of Matthew in its Roman Imperial Context* (Riches J and Sim DC, Editors). T & T Clark, New York.

Eugene EL (1991). *The Past of Jesus in the Gospels*. Cambridge University Press, Cambridge.

Faber-Kaiser A (1976). *Jesus Died in Kashmir: Jesus, Moses and the 10 Lost Tribes of Israel*. Gordon and Cremonisi, Ltd., London.

Farmer WR (1976). *The Synoptic Problem*, 2nd Edition. Mercer University Press, Macon.

Farquhar JN (1927). *The Apostle Thomas in South India*. Manchester University Press, Manchester.

Farrar DFW (1874). *The Life of Christ*. London.

Farrer A (1955). *On Dispensing With Q. Studies in the Gospels: Essays in Memory of R. H. Lightfoot* (Nineham DE, Editor). Blackwell, Oxford.

Fawcett L and Greenwood BJ (1984). *Clear Intent: The Government Coverup of the UFO Experience*. Prentice-Hall, Englewood Cliffs, NJ.

Ferrier JP (1858). *History of the Afghans* (translated from unpublished manuscript by Capt. W. Jesse). John Murray, London.

Flusser D (1968). *Jesus in Selbstzeugnissen und Bilddokumenten.* Hamburg.

Forster G (1808). *A Journey from Bengal to England, through the Northern Part of India, Kashmire, Afghanistan, and Perisa, and into Russia by the Caspian-Sea,* Volume II. R. Faulder and Son, London.

Geiselman JR (1951). *Jesus der Christus.* Stuttgart.

Ghulam Ahmad and Hazrat Mirza (1908). *Masih Hindustan mein (Urdu).* Qadian, Pakistan.

Ghulam Ahmad and Hazrat Mirza (1962). *Jesus in India.* Ahmadiyya Muslim Foreign Missions Department, Rabwah, Pakistan.

Gillabert E (1974). *Paroles de Jésus et Pensée Orientale.* Éditions Métanoia, Marsanne, Montélimar.

Goddard D (1927). *Was Jesus Influenced by Buddhism?* Thetford, Vermont

Goguel M (1950). *Jesus.* Paris.

Good T (1988). *Above Top Secret: The Worldwide UFO Cover-up.* William Morrow, New York.

Goodacre M (1998). Fatigue in the Synoptics. *New Testament Studies* 44, 45-58.

Goodacre M (2002). *The Case Against Q: Studies in Markan Priority and Synoptic Problem.* Trinity Press International, Harrisburg, PA.

References

Goodman M (1987). *The Ruling Class of Judaea.* Cambridge University Press, Cambridge.

Goodspeed J (1959). *Matthew: Apostle and Evangelist.* John Winston Co., Philadelphia.

Gordon S (1984). Update on the Bellwood, Pennsylvania UFO car lift case. *MUFON UFO Journal.* 200 (Dec).

Gordon S (1985). Penn State Sighting. *MUFON UFO Journal.* 212(Dec).

Gore C and Leighton H (1928). *A New Commentary on the Holy Scriptures, Including the Apocrypha.* Thornton and Butterworth, London.

Gorion E, Editor (1962). *Die Sagen der Juden.* Frankfurt.

Goulder MD (1974). *Midrash and Lection in Matthew.* Society for Promoting Christian Knowledge, London.

Goulder MD (1989). *Luke – A New Paradigm, Volumes I and II.* Journal for the Study of the Old Testament Press, Sheffield, England.

Goulder MD (1996). Is Q a Juggernaut? *Journal of Biblical Literature* 115, 667-681.

Grant M (1967). *Herod the Great.* J.B. Lippincott Co., New York.

Graves R and Podro J (1957). *Jesus in Rome.* Cassell & Company, London.

Greer S (1999). *Extraterrestrial Contact: The Evidence and Implications.* Crossing Point, Inc. Publications, Afton, VA.

Greg W (1907). *The Creed of Christendom*. Macmillan, London.

Gregory A (1907). *The Canon and Text of the New Testament*. New York.

Guignebert C (1935). *Le Monde juif vers le temps de Jésus*. Paris.

Guthrie D (1965). *New Testament Introduction*. Inter-Varsity Press, Downers Grove, IL.

Guthrie D (1970). *New Testament Introduction*, 3rd Edition. Inter-Varsity Press, Downers Grove.

Haag H (1951). Bibel-Lexikon. Based on Bijbelsch Woordenboek (van den Born A, Editor), 1941. *Spanish edition: de Ausejo S, Editor (1967). Diccionario de la Biblia*. Barcelona.

Haenchen E (1968). *Der Weg Jesu*. Berlin.

Haig TW (1928). *The Kingdom of Kashmir*. Cambridge University Press, Cambridge.

Hanna W (1928). *The Life of Christ*. American Tract Society, New York.

Harrison ER (1981). *Cosmology*. Cambridge University Press, New York.

Hassnain F (1994). *A Search for the Historical Jesus*. Gateway Books, Bath, England.

Head P (1997). *Christology and the Synoptic Problem: An Argument for Markan Priority*. Cambridge University Press, Cambridge.

References

Headland AC (1914). *The Miracles of the New Testament.* Longman Green, London.

Hengel M (1961). *Die Zeloten.* Leiden.

Hirn Y (1912). *The Sacred Shrine.* Macmillan, London.

Hodson G (n.d.). *The Christ Life from Nativity to Ascension.* Theosophical Publishing House, Illinois.

Hoehner HW (1972). *Herod Antipas.* Zondervan Pub. House, Grand Rapids, MI.

Holt JC (1991). *Buddha in the Crown.* Oxford University Press, New York.

Holtzmann HJ (1863). *Die synoptischen Evangelien.* Leipzig.

Horne TH (1823). *An Introduction to the Critical Study and Knowledge of the Holy Scriptures* (Alford H, Editor), 4th Edition, Volume 4. London.

Horsley R (1989). *Sociology and the Jesus Movement.* Crossroad, New York.

Hubbard BJ (1981). In review of The Vision of Matthew by John P. Meier. *Journal of Biblical Literature* 100, 121-122.

Hugh J (1839). *History of Christians in India from the Commencement of the Christian Era.* Seeley and Burnside, London.

Instinsky HU (1957). *Das Jahr der Geburt Jesu.* Munich.

I-Tsing (1896). *A Record of The Buddhist Religion as Practised in India and the Malay Archipelago (A.D. 671-695)* (Takakusu J, Translator). Clarendon Press, Oxford.

James P (1983). Did Christ die in Kashmir? *Islamic Review* 3(Oct/Nov), 17.

Jameson HG (1922). *The Origin of the Synoptic Gospels*. Blackwell, Oxford.

Jawarhar Lal Nehru (1942). *Glimpses of World History*. John Day Co., New York.

Jeremias J (1958). *Jerusalem der Zeit Jesu*. Göttingen.

Jeremias J (1966). *Studien zur neutestamentlichen Theologie und Zeitgeschichte*. Göttingen.

Jeremias J (1970). *Die Gleichnisse Jesu*. Göttingen.

John W (1895). Journey to Kashmir, in *Asiatic Researches*. Baptist Mission Press, Calcutta.

Johnston AK (1855). *Dictionary of Geography, Descriptive, Physical, Statistical, And Historical, Forming a Complete General Gazetteer of the World, 2nd Edition*. Longman, Brown, Green, and Longman, London.

Josephus, *Antiquities* XVII, xii, par. 2, and beginning of XVIII.

Josephus F (1840). *The Works of Flavius Josephus; comprising the Antiquities of the Jews; a History of the Jewish Wars, and Life of Flavius Josephus* (Whiston W, Translator). Willoughby & Co., London.

References

Joyce D (1972). *The Jesus Scroll*. Ferret Books, Melbourne.

Kahler M (1969). *Der sogennante historische Jesus und der geschichtliche, biblische Christus*. Wolf, Munich.

Kak RB and Pandit Ram Chand (1933). *Ancient Monuments of Kashmir*. India Society, London.

Kamal-ud-Din, Al-Haj Hazrat Khwaja (1921). *Islam and Christianity*. MM and L Trust, Woking, Surrey.

Kamal-ud-Din and Al-Haj Hazrat Khwaja (1922). *The Sources of Christianity*. MM and L Trust, Woking, Surrey.

Kamal-ud-Din and Al-Haj Hazrat Khwaja (1932). *A Running Commentary on the Holy Qur'an*. MM and L Trust, Woking, Surrey.

Kasemann, E (1964). *Exegetische Versuche und Besinnung*. Göttingen.

Kaul PA (1913). *The Geography of Jammu and Kashmir*. Thacker, Spink and Co., Calcutta.

Kaul PA (1924). *The Kashmir Pandits*. Thacker, Spink and Co., Calcutta.

Kautsky K (1908). *Der Ursprung des Christentums*. Stuttgart.

Kautzsch E, Editor (1900). *Die Apokryphen und Pseudepigraphen des Alten Testaments*. Tübingen.

Kehimkar HS (1937). *Bani Israel of India*. Dayag Press, Tel Aviv.

Keller W (1955). *Und die Bibel hat doch recht*. Dusseldorf.

Kennett RH (1933). *Ancient Hebrew Social Life and Customs as indicated in Law, Narrative and Metaphor.* Oxford University Press, Oxford.

Kenyon F (1939). *Our Bible and the Ancient Manuscripts, Being a History of the Texts and Translations.* Eyre and Spottiswoode, London.

Kersten H (1986). *Jesus Lived in India* (Woods-Czisch T, Translator). Element Book, Longmead, Shaftesbury, Dorset, England.

Kersten H (2001). *Jesus Lived in India: His Unknown Life Before and After the Crucifixion.* Penguin, New Delhi, India.

Khaniyari MGMN (n.d.). *Wajeez-ut-Tawarikh.* Research Library, Srinagar.

Khwaja Nazir Ahmad (n.d.). *Jesus in Heaven on Earth.* Woking Muslim Mission & Literary Trust, Woking, England.

Khwand M (1891). *Rauzat-us-Safa* (Rehatsek E, Translator). Arbuthnot, MRAS, London.

Kinder G (1987). *Light Years: An Investigation into the Extraterrestrial Experiences of Eduard Meier.* Atlantic Monthly Press, New York.

Klausner J (1925). *Jesus of Nazareth.* Allen and Unwin, London.

Klijn AFJ (1962). *The Acts of Thomas.* Brill, Leiden.

Knowles J, Editor (1984). *The Nineteenth Century: a Monthly Review, Vol. XXXVI (Jul-Dec).* Sampson Low, Marston & Co., London.

Kroll G (1963). *Auf den Spuren Jesu.* Leipzig.

References

Kuiper TBH and Morris, M (1977). Searching for extraterrestrial civilizations. *Science* 196, 616-621.

Kümmel WG (1966). *Introduction to the New Testament*. Abingdon Press, Nashville.

Kung, H (1974). *Christ sein*. Peper, Munich.

Lake K (1907). *The Historical Evidence for the Resurrection of Jesus Christ*. London.

Lauenstein D (1971). *Der Messias*. Stuttgart.

Lawrence W (1895). *The Valley of Kashmir*. Froude, London.

Lehmann J (1970). *Jesus-Report. Protokoll einer Verfälschung*. Düsseldorf.

Leipoldt J (1920). *Hat Jesus gelebt?* Leipzig.

Lewis SH (1929). *Mystical Life of Jesus*. Supreme Grand Lodge of Ancient Mystical Order Rosae Crucis, San Jose, California.

Loewenthal I (1865). *Some Persian Inscriptions Found in Kashmir*. Asiatic Society of Bengal, Calcutta.

Lohse E (1964). *Die Texte aus Qumran*. Kösel.

Lopez DS and Rockefeller SC, Editors (1987). T*he Christ and the Bodhisattva*. State University of New York Press, New York.

Lord JH (1907). *The Jews in India and the Far East*. Society for Promoting Christian Knowledge, Bombay.

Maccabee B (1989a). Pendulum from the Pleiades. *International UFO Reporter* 14(1, Jan/Feb), 11-12, 22.

Maccabee B (1989b). Pleiades Pendulum (Response). *International UFO Reporter* 14(5), 21-24.

Maccabee B (1993). Gulf Breeze lights still unexplained. *International UFO Reporter* 18(1, Jan/Feb), 20.

Maccabee B (2000). *UFO FBI Connection*. Llewellyn Publications, St. Paul, MN.

Macdonald G (1904). The pseudo-autonomous coinage of Antioch. *Numismatic Chronicle* 4(IV), 105-135.

Mack B (1991). *A Myth of Innocence: Mark and Christian Origins*. Fortress Press, Philadelphia.

Maier J (1960). *Die Texte vom Toten Meer*. Munich.

Malleson GB (1879). *History of Afghanistan: from the Earliest Period to the Outbreak of the War of 1878*. W.H. Allen & Co., London.

Mann CS (1986). *The Anchor Bible: Mark, Volume 27*. Doubleday & Co., New York.

Marxen W (1964). *Einleitung in das Neue Testament*. Gütersloh, Munich.

Marxen W (1965). *Die Auferstehung Jesu als historisches und theologisches Problem*. Gütersloh, Munich.

Maulvi Muhammad Ali (1936). *The Religion of Islam*. Ahmadiyya Anjuman Isha'at-i-Islam, Lahore.

References

Maulvi Muhammad Ali (1945). *History of the Prophets*. Ahmadiyya Anjuman Isha'at-i-Islam, Lahore.

McCasland SV (1932). *The Resurrection of Jesus*. Nelson, London.

McKnight S (2001). *A generation who knew not Streeter. Rethinking the Synoptic Problem* (Black DA and Beck DR, Editors). Baker Academic, Grand Rapids, MI.

McNeile AH (1915). *The Gospel According to St. Matthew*. Macmillan & Co., London.

Meffert F (1920). *Die geschichtliche Existenz Christi*. Münchengladbach.

Meier E (ca. 1983). *Verzeichnis: Authentischer Farb-Photos*. E. Meier, Hinterschmidrüti, Switzerland.

Meier E, Editor (2001). *The Talmud of Jmmanuel*. Wild Flower Press, Mill Spring, NC.

Merrick, HS (1931). *In the World's Attic*. Putnam, London.

Meyer A (1909). *Jesus or Paul* (Wilkinson FA, Translator). Harper, London.

Milligan W (1905). *The Resurrection of Our Lord*. Macmillan, London.

Mir Khawand bin Badshah (1852). *Rauza-tus-Safa (The Gardens of Purity)*, Volume I of VII. Bombay.

Molnar MR (2000). *The Star of Bethlehem*. Rutgers University Press, New Brunswick, NJ.

Monier-Williams, M (1890). *Buddhism, in its Connexion with Brahmanism and Hinduism, and in its Contrast with Christianity*, 2nd Edition. John Murray, London.

Moore G (1861). *The Lost Tribes and the Saxons of the East and of the West, with new Views of Buddhism, and Translations of Rock-Records in India*. Longman, Green, Longman, and Roberts, London.

Mozundar AK (1917). *Hindu History (3000 BC to 1200 AD)*. Dacca.

Nazir Ahmad and Al-Haj Khwaja (1973). *Jesus in Heaven on Earth*. Azeez Manzil, Lahore.

New DS (1997). *Old Testament Quotations in the Synoptic Gospels and the Two-Document Hypothesis*. Scholars Press, Atlanta, GA.

Newman W and Sagan C (1981). Galactic civilizations: Population dynamics and interstellar diffusion. *Icarus* 46, 296.

Noerlinger HS (1957). *Moses und Ägypten*. Heidelberg.

Notovich N (1894). *The Unknown Life of Jesus Christ* (translated from French edition by Loranger H). Rand McNally, Chicago.

O'Neill JC (1974-75). The Synoptic Problem. *New Testament Studies* 21, 273f.

Oldenberg H (1882). *Buddha: His Life, His Doctrine, His Order* (Hoey W, Translator). Williams and Norgate, London.

Olsen TM (1989). Pleiades pendulum (Letter). *International UFO Reporter* 14(5, Sept/Oct), 24.

Otto R (1940). *Reich Gottes und Menschensohn*. Munich.

References

Palmer EH (1880). *The Qur'an. Sacred Books of the East series.* Clarendon Press, Oxford.

Pande KC (1936). *Abhinavagupta: An Historical and Philosophical Study.* Benares.

Pannenberg W (1964). *Grundzüge der Christologie.* Gütersloh, Munich.

Parker P (1983). *The Posteriority of Mark. New Synoptic Studies* (Farmer WR, Editor). Mercer University Press, Macon, GA.

Patton CS (1915). *Sources of the Synoptic Gospels.* The Macmillan Company, London.

Pearson BA (1990). *Gnosticism, Judaism, and Egyptian Christianity.* Fortress Press, Minneapolis.

Pine C (1993). Current Cases. *MUFON UFO Journal* 305 (Sept), 20.

Prinsep H. T. (1852). *Tibet, Tartary and Mongolia; their Social and Political Condition, and the Religion of Boodh, as there Existing, 2nd Edition.* William H. Allen Co., London.

Ragg L and LM (1907). *The Gospel of Barnabas.* Clarendon Press, Oxford.

Ramsay W (1905). *Was Christ born in Bethlehem?* Hodder and Stoughton, London.

Rangacharya V (1937). *History of Pre-Musulman India.* Indian Publishing House, Madras.

Rapson EJ (1911). *Ancient India*. Cambridge University Press, Cambridge.

Ray HC (1931). *The Dynastic History of Northern India*, Volumes I and II. Thacker, Spink and Co., Calcutta.

Ray SC (1969). *Early History and Culture of Kashmir*. Munshiram Manoharlal, New Delhi.

Reicke B (1965). *Newtestamentliche Zeitgeschichte*. Göttingen.

Reidmann A (1951). *Die Wahrheit des Christentums*. Freiburg im Breisgau.

Reilson W (1927). *History of Afghanistan*. John Rylands Library Bulletin.

Rengstorf KH (1955). *Die Auferstehung Jesu*. Berlin.

Rhys Davids CAF (1912). *Buddhism*. Williams, London.

Rhys Davids TW (1881). *Lectures on the Origin and Growth of Religion as Illustrated by some Points in the History of Indian Buddhism. The Hibbert Lectures, 1881*. Williams and Norgate, London.

Rhys Davids TW (1882). *Buddhism: being a Sketch of the Life and Teachings of Gautama, the Buddha*. Society for Promoting Christian Knowledge, London.

Rhys Davids TW (1896). *Buddhism, its History and Literature*. Putnam, New York.

Rietmüller O (1922). *Woher wissen wir, dass Jesus gelebt hat?* Stuttgart.

References

Ristow H and Matthiae K (1961). *Der geschichtliche Jesus und der Kerygmatische Christus*. Berlin.

Roberts A and Donaldson J (Eds.) (1956). *Eusebius, Ecumenical History (EH) 3.39.16. The Ante-Nicene Fathers (ANF)*, Volume I. Eerdmans, Grand Rapids.

Roberts A and Donaldson J (Editors) (1993). *Ignatius, Epistle to the Ephesians. The Ante-Nicene Fathers (ANF), Volume I.* Eerdmans Publishing Company, Grand Rapids.

Robinson F (1902). *The Coptic Apocryphal Gospels*. Methuen, London.

Robinson JM (1959). *The New Quest of the Historical Jesus*. London.

Robinson TA (1988). *The Bauer Thesis Examined: The Geography of Heresy in the Early Christian Church*. Edwin Mellen Press, Lewiston, New York.

Rockhill WW (1884). *The Life of the Buddha and the Early History of his Order. Derived from Tibetan Works in the Bkah-Hgyur and Bstan-Hgyur.* Trübner & Company, London.

Rodgers, RW (1929). *A History of Ancient India*. Scribner, London.

Rose GH (1852). *The Afghans: The Ten Tribes and the Kings of the East*. Operative Jewish Converts Institution Press, London.

Sanders EP (1985). *Jesus and Judaism*. Fortress Press, Philadelphia.

Schelke KH (1949). *Die Passion Jesu in der Verkundigüng des Neuen Testaments*. Heidelberg.

Schelke KH (1960). *Die Gemeinde von Qumran und die Kirche des Neuen Testaments. Die Welt der Bibel.* Düsseldorf.

Schick E (1940). *Formgeschichte und Synoptiker Exegese.* Münster.

Schmidt KL (1919). *Der Rahmen der Geschichte Jesu.* Berlin.

Scholem G (1973). *Von der mystischen Gestalt der Gottheit.* Frankfurt.

Schonfield HJ (1966). *The Passover Plot.* Hutchinson, London.

Schubert K (1962). *Der historische Jesus und der Christus unseres Glaubens.* Vienna.

Schubert K (1964). *Vom Messias zum Christus.* Vienna and Freiburg.

Schurer E (1901-9). *Geschichte des jüdischen Volker im Zeitalter Jesu Christi.* Leipsiz.

Schwegler T (1962). *Die Biblische Urgeschichte.* Munich.

Schweitzer A (1901). *Das Messianitäts-und Leidensgeheimnis.* Tübingen.

Schweitzer A (1966). *Geschichte der Leben-Jesu-Forschung.* Munich.

Schweitzer E (1968). *Jesus Christus im vielfaltigen Zeugnis des Neuen Testaments.* Munich and Hamburg.

Seydel R (1880). *Das Evangelium von Jesu in Seinem Verhältnissen zu Buddhas Sage und Buddhas Lehre.* Leipzig.

Shaikh A-Said-us-Sadiq (1782). *Kamal-ud-Din.* Syed-us-Sanad Press, Iran.

References

Shams JD (1945). *Where Did Jesus Die?* Baker and Witt, London.

Simon M (1960). *Les Sectes juives au temps de Jésus.* Paris.

Sinclair M (1887). *Countess of Caithness. The Mystery of the Ages contained in the Secret Doctrine of all Religions.* Wallace CLH, Philanthropic Reform Publisher, Oxford Mansion, W., London.

Smith VA (1966). *Akbar the Great Mogul, 1542-1605.* S. Chand, Dehli.

Smith GB (1922). *A Guide to the Study of the Christian Religion.* Chicago University Press, Chicago.

Smith RG (1937). *Early Relations between India and Iran.* London.

Smith VA (1904). *The Early History of India.* Clarendon Press, Oxford.

Soter S (1985). The cosmic quarantine hypothesis. *Planetary Report* 5, 20-21.

Sprinkle RL (1999). *Soul Samples: Personal Explorations in Reincarnation and UFO Experiences.* Granite Publishing, Columbus, NC.

Stanton WH (1927). *The Gospels as Historical Documents.* Cambridge University Press, Cambridge.

Stauffer E (1957). *Jesus, Gestalt and Geschichte.* Bern.

Stein MA, Translator (1900). *Kalhana's Chronicle of the Kings of Kashmir, Volumes I and II.* London.

Stein RH (1987). *The Synoptic Problem: An Introduction*. Baker Book House, Grand Rapids, MI.

Stein RH (1992). The Matthew-Luke Agreements against Mark: Insight from John. *Catholic Biblical Quarterly* 54, 482-502.

Stevens WC (1982). UFO Contact from the Pleiades: A Preliminary Investigation Report. *UFO Photo Archives* (out of print), Tucson.

Stevens WC (1988). Message from the Pleiades, Volume I. *UFO Photo Archives* (out of print), Tucson.

Strauss DF (1835-6). *Das Leben Jesu, kritich bearbeitet*. Tübingen.

Strauss DF (1879). *A New Life of Jesus, Volume I*. Williams and Norgate, London.

Streeter BH (1924). *The Four Gospels: A Study of Origins*. Macmillan and Co., London.

Stroud W (1905). *On the Physical Cause of Death of Christ*. Hamilton and Adams, London.

Styler GM (1982). The Priority of Mark, in Moule CFD, *The Birth of the New Testament*, Excursis IV, 3rd Edition. Harper and Row, San Francisco.

Sufi GMD (1974). *Kashmir, being a History of Kashmir from the Earliest Times*, Volumes I and II. Light and Life Publishers, New Delhi and Jammu.

Sumi TD, Oki M and Hassnain FM (1975). *Ladakh, the Moonland*. Light and Life Publishers, New Delhi, Jammu and Rothak.

References

Sutta P (1917). *Bhavishya Maha Puranan*. Venkateshvaria Press, Bombay.

Thiering B (1992). *Jesus and the Riddle of the Dead Sea Scrolls*. Harper SanFrancisco, San Francisco.

Thomas EJ (1951). *The History of Buddhist Thought, 2nd Edition*. Barnes & Noble, New York.

Thomas L'Évangile selon (1975). *Éditions Métanoia*, Marsanne, Montélimar.

Thomas P (1973). *Epics, Myths and Legends of India, 13th Edition*. Taraporevala, Bombay.

Tola, F (1973). *Doctrinas secretas de la India Upanishads*. Barral, Barcelona.

Trocmé É (1971). *Jésus de Nazareth vu par les témoins de so vie*. Delaclaux et Nestlé, Neuchâtel.

Tuckett CM (1983a). 1 Corinthians and Q. *Journal of Biblical Literature* 102, 607-619.

Tuckett CM (1983b). *The Revival of the Griesbach Hypothesis*. Cambridge University Press, New York.

Tuckett CM (1992). *The Synoptic Problem. The Anchor Bible Dictionary, Vol. 6* (Freedman DN, Editor). Doubleday, New York.

Tuckett CM (1996). *Q and the History of Early Christianity*. Hendrickson, Peabody, MA.

Verus SE (1897). *Vergleichende Übersichtder vier Evangelien*. Leipzig.

Vigne GT (1840). *A personal narrative of a visit to Ghuzni, Kabul, and Afghanistan, and of a Residence at the Court of Dost Mohamed: with Notices of Runjit Sing, Khiva, and the Russian Expedition.* Whittaker & Co., London.

Vogtle A (1964). *Exegetische Erwägungen über das Wissen und Selbstbewusstsein Jesu.* Freiburg im Breisgau.

von Campenhausen H (1958). *Der Ablauf der Osterereignisse und das leere Grab.* Heidelberg.

von Harnack A (1964). *Das Wesen des Christentums.* Munich.

Waddell LA (1975). *Lhasa and its Mysteries.* Sanskaran Prakashak, New Delhi.

Walters E and Maccabee, B (1997). *UFOs Are Real: Here's the Proof.* Avon Books, New York.

Warechaner J (1927). *The Historical Life of Christ.* London.

Weigall A (1916). *Paganism in our Christianity.* Hutchinson, London.

Weiss J (1892-1900). *Die Predigt Jesu vom Reiche Gottes.* Göttingen.

Whitney D (1906). *The Resurrection of the Lord.* Hamilton and Adams, London.

Williams M (1889). *Buddhism.* Macmillan, New York.

Wilson HH (1841). *History of Kashmir*, in Asiatic Researches. Baptist Mission Press, Calcutta.

References

Wolff J (1845). *Narrative of a Mission to Bokhara, in the years 1843-1845, to ascertain the Fate of Colonel Stoddart and Captain Conolly*, Volume 1, 2nd Edition, (J.W. Parker, rev.). London.

Wood HG (1953-54). The Priority of Mark. *Expository Times* 65, pp.17-19.

Wright D (1943). *Studies in Islam and Christianity*. MM and L Trust, Woking, Surrey.

Wright W (1871). *The Apocryphal Acts of the Apostles*. Williams and Norgate, London.

Wuenshel E (1954). *Self Portrait of Christ*. New York.

Yasin M (1972). *Mysteries of Kashmir*. Kesar, Srinagar.

Younghusband F (1909). *Kashmir*. Black, London.

Zahn T (1909). *Introduction to the New Testament*, Volume 2. T. & T. Clark, Edinburgh.

Zahrnt H (1969). *Es Begann mit Jesus von Nazareth*. Gütersloh, Munich.

Zimmermann H (1973). *Jesus Christus: Geschichte und Verkündigung*. Stuttgart.

Zimmern H (1910). *Zum Streit um die "Christus Mythe."* Berlin.

Zockler O, Editor (1891). *Die Apokryphen des Alten Testaments*. Munich.

www.ingramcontent.com/pod-product-compliance
Lightning Source LLC
Chambersburg PA
CBHW021449080526
44588CB00009B/764